THE WAE OF EMOTIONS

JACOB TRIGG

ILLUSTRATED BY
VALENTINA DAVILA

The WAE of Emotions

Copyright @ 2023
Jacob Trigg

Illustrated by Valentina Davila

YGTMedia Co. Press Trade Paperback Edition

Published in Canada,
for Global Distribution by YGTMedia Co.

www.ygtmedia.co/publishing

ISBN 978-1-998754-17-5 Paperback
ISBN 978-1-998754-18-2 Hardcover

All Rights Reserved. No part of this book can be scanned, distributed, or copied without permission. This book or any portion thereof may not be reproduced or used in any manner whatsoever without the express written permission of the publisher at publishing@ygtmedia.co
—except for the use of brief quotations in a book review.

Printed in North America

DEDICATION
TO ALL THE FEELS

COMMUNITY IS THE KEY TO UNITY

ONCE UPON A TIME

there was a boy named Jake. He was always curious about the nature of things. He also often had strong feelings and emotions.

MOST OF THE TIME JAKE FELT JOY.

Sometimes, though, Jake had other emotions he didn't like so much. Sometimes he felt sad. Sometimes he felt angry. Sometimes he felt scared or ashamed.

He wasn't sure where these feelings came from. Sometimes it was because something bad had happened, like the time he dropped his ice cream. He was so sad about that.

And sometimes the feelings seemed to come from out of nowhere, like the time he felt scared before bedtime. Or on the day he was angry in the morning before school.

JAKE WASN'T SURE WHAT TO DO ABOUT THESE FEELINGS.

As he grew, the feelings got bigger and started becoming more powerful. He couldn't think normally when these feelings came up. He was overwhelmed. And sometimes he felt like he wasn't in control.

One ritual that Jake and his dad practiced was a special time for questions and answers. They called this Q&A time. During Q&A time, Jake could ask his dad any question, and his dad would share answers.

"Dad, where do emotions come from? Why do we have emotions? And what should we do with them?" Jake asked.

"Those are big questions, Jake," his dad said. "I will tell you the secret to emotions. But first you need to understand the WAE of emotions. Listen closely as I tell you the story."

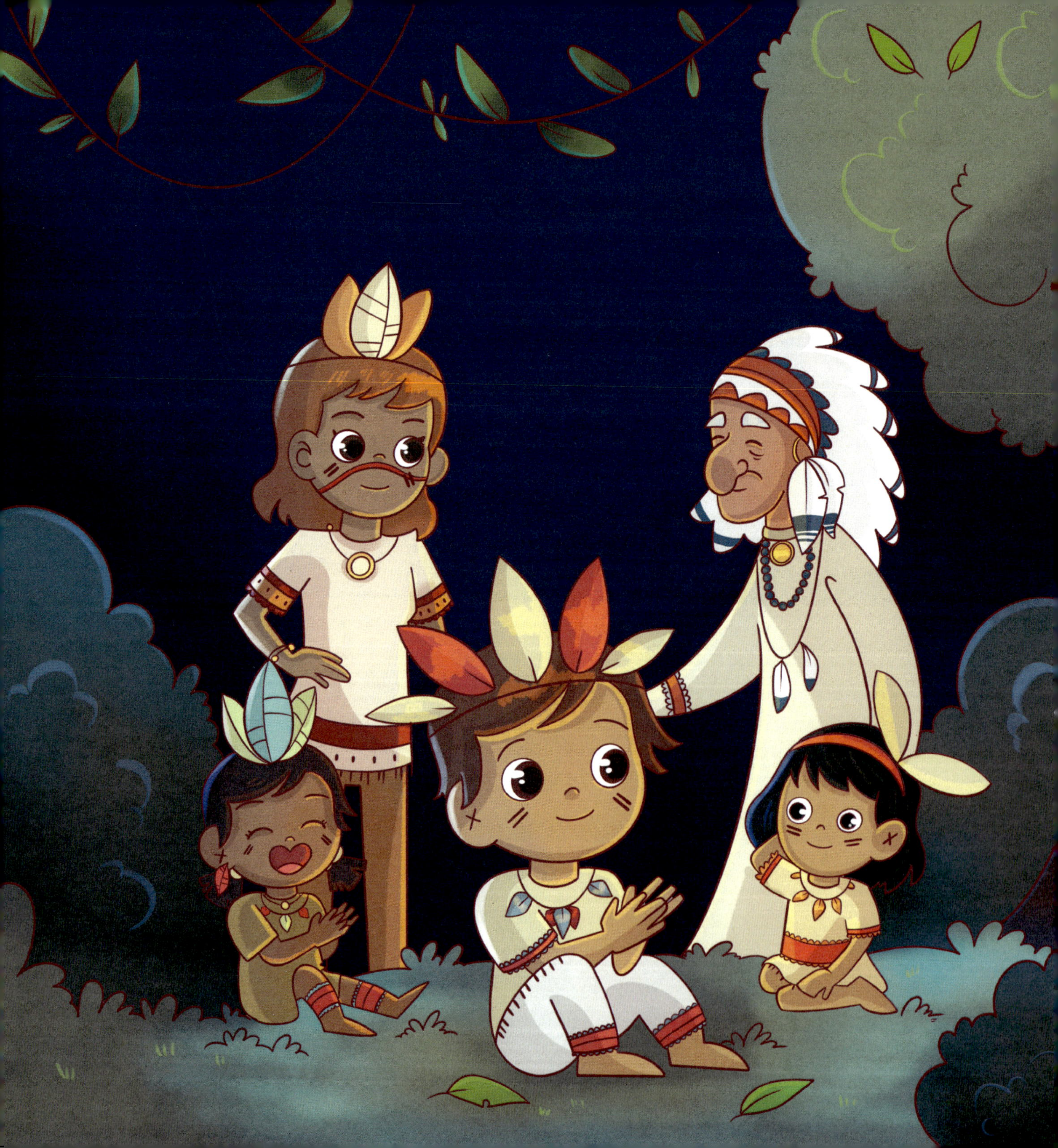

A LONG, LONG TIME AGO THERE WAS A BOY.

He lived in the jungle with his parents
and brothers and cousins and an entire tribe.

The tribe had a ritual for emotions.
They called this the WAE of emotions.

It goes like this.

INITIAL LESSON:
PART OF ME FEELS LIKE . . .

Whenever the moon was most full or empty of light,
the tribe would gather and talk about the WAE.
One of the elders always started the tale the same way:

"Children, fathers and mothers, listen. This is the WAE.
What's most important about the WAE is to recognize that
only a part of you feels a certain way. A part of you can feel
sad. A part of you can feel happy. A part of you can feel angry.

You are not the sadness, even though
it may feel like it at the time.

These emotional parts are ancient. They are gifts
that humans received even before we had language.

Emotions help us to know when we are in danger, such as
fear. They also help us to know what is important to us, such
as sadness when we lose something or miss someone.

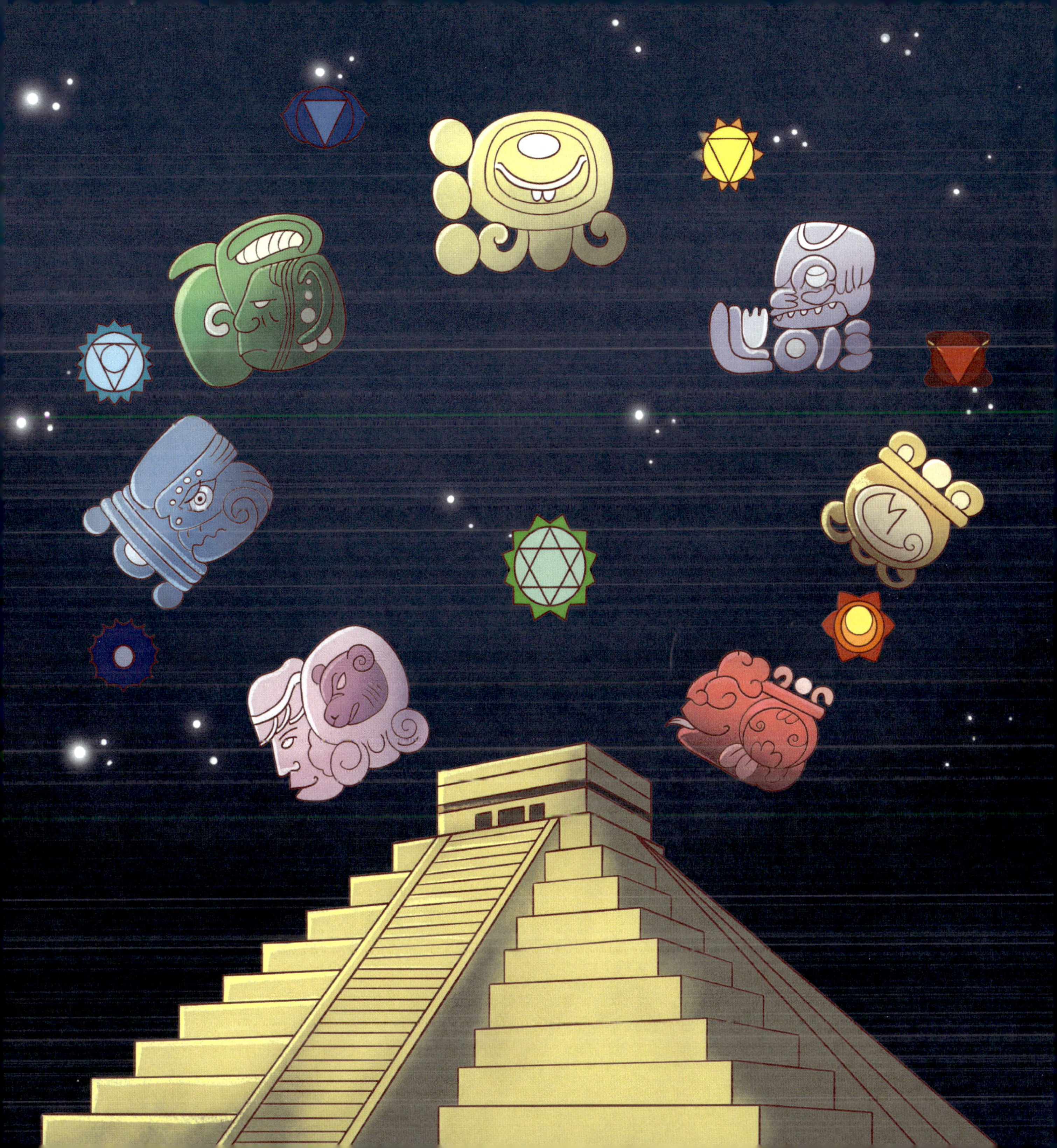

These emotions are energy, just like the rest of our body and our thoughts. It's important to allow this energy to move through us. To really feel, allow, and express the emotions.

Because if we don't listen to and release the emotions, they become stuck. Emotions don't like being stuck, so they will do all kinds of things to be free. You don't want to be at the mercy of an unexpressed emotion.

NOW, LET US PRACTICE THE WAE.

Who would like to go first?
Who is feeling something strongly
but may not understand it or know what to do?"

The boy raises his hand.

STEP 1: WITNESS OR WATCH THE EMOTION

The first step of the WAE of emotions is to watch or witness the feeling.

"What does the feeling or emotion look like?
What does it sound like?
Where is it in your body?" the elder asks.

"Hmm," the boy ponders.
"I feel sad in my heart. It's blue."

"Good," the elder says. "Part of you feels blue sadness in your heart. Does it have a texture or weight? Is it sticky or soft? Heavy or light?"

"It's heavy and sticky."

"Good," the elder says. "Part of you feels sad. It's blue, heavy, sticky, and in your heart. Is there anything else about this sad part? Does it want to say anything else?"

"It is telling me that I miss my mom. We don't get to play as often as I would like," says the boy.

"Wonderful!" exclaims the elder.
"Thank you, sadness, for revealing where you come from!
Now, if this sadness were an animal, what would it be?"

"Hmm," the boy thinks. "I guess it would be a bird."

"What kind of bird?"

"A raven."

"Perfect. Now picture this raven and we will invite this raven into Step 2 of the WAE."

STEP 2: ACCEPT THE EMOTION. EVERYTHING ELSE IS OKAY.

"Boy, can you accept this sad, blue, and sticky raven for what he brings?"

"I don't want to, really. The raven is scary to me."

"Good! The raven is showing you another part. Can you tell why the raven is scary?"

"Because the raven is angry. He wants to play, but he isn't allowed to. He is hungry and just wants to play."

"Wonderful. Now, aside from this raven being sad, scary, angry, and hungry, is everything else okay?"

"Hmm, I guess so. The raven is sad, scary, angry, and hungry, but that's it. Everything else is okay. He still has friends. He still has a family and other ravens to play and learn with as well as nature to enjoy."

"Okay, now I want you to think about if you can accept the raven for exactly what it is: blue, sticky, sad, scary, angry, and hungry."

"Yes, I see the raven as it is and that's okay. I can accept this raven."

The raven and the boy hug.

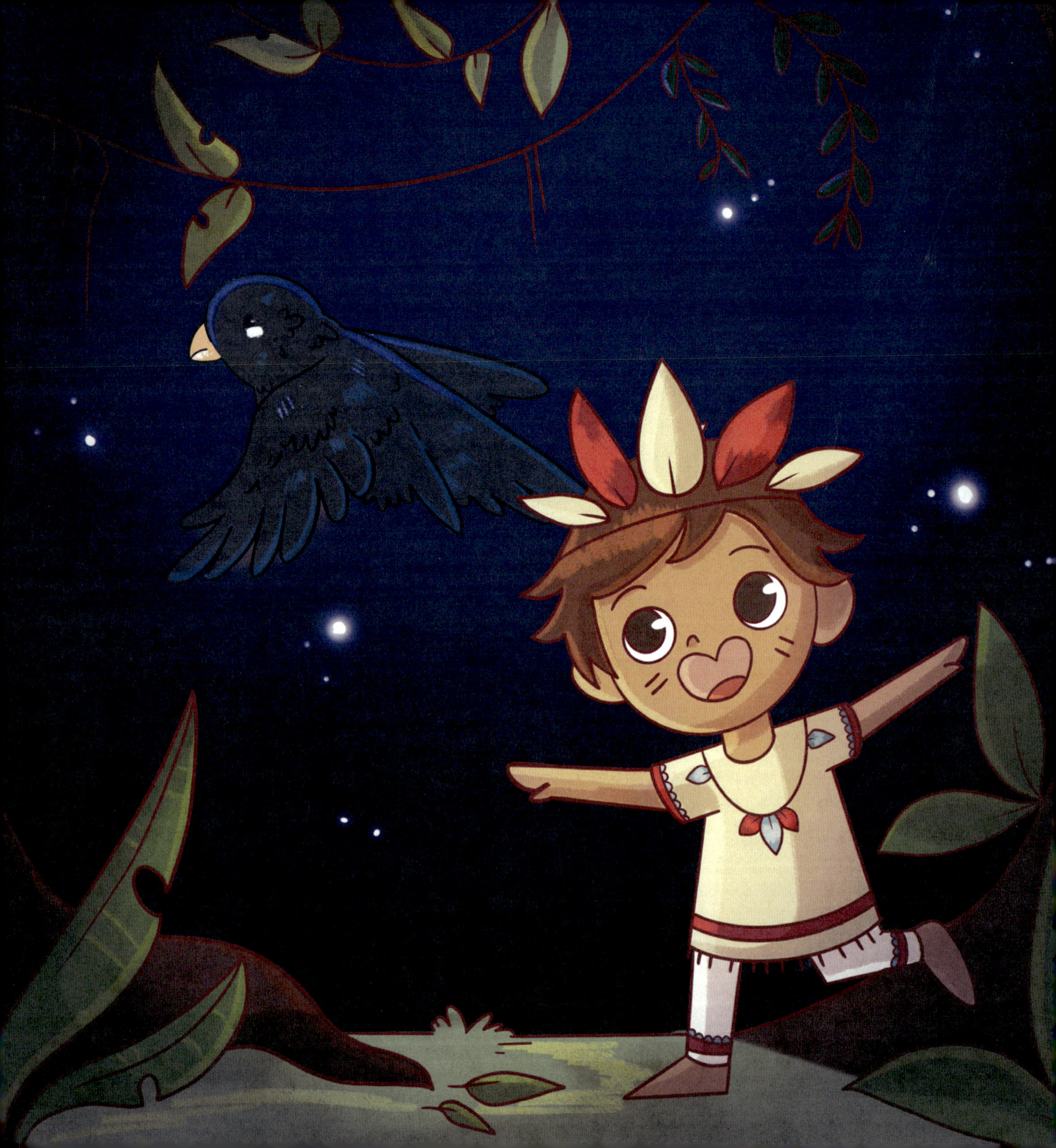

STEP 3: EXPRESS THE EMOTION

"Perfect! Now you are ready for the final step of the WAE. It is time to express the emotions.

There are many ways to express them, but one of the best ways is to dance. How does the raven dance?

If this raven could make a noise or move to show how it feels, what would that look and sound like?"

The boy spreads his arms out wide and starts moving around the circle. He flaps his arms as if flying.

Caw! Caw! Caw!

The boy feels so alive!
He pretends to be a raven flying around the tribe.

But then he remembers this raven is sad, angry, and hungry. That's when the boy feels tears coming. But he doesn't want to cry in front of the tribe.

His mother stands up and joins the boy. She pretends to be a raven and flies next to his side.

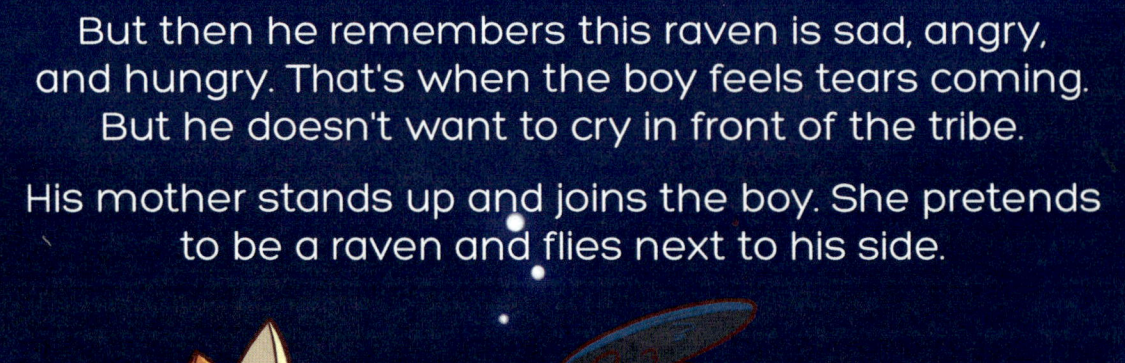

He sees her and can no longer hold back the tears.

His mother places her wings around him. She holds him close as he cries.

Then the boy pushes his mother away! He is mad at her because she didn't play with him the day before.

"Good!" says the elder. "Express the anger."

"Ah!" the boy yells. "Mom, I just wanted to play yesterday, but you said it was time to eat. I didn't want to eat. I wanted to play!"

The mother simply watches the boy. She doesn't say anything, but he can feel her love.

The boy stamps his feet and yells some more. The tribe does not move. Many of them even start to smile. They smile because the boy is practicing the WAE so well. He is welcoming, accepting, and expressing the complex web of emotions.

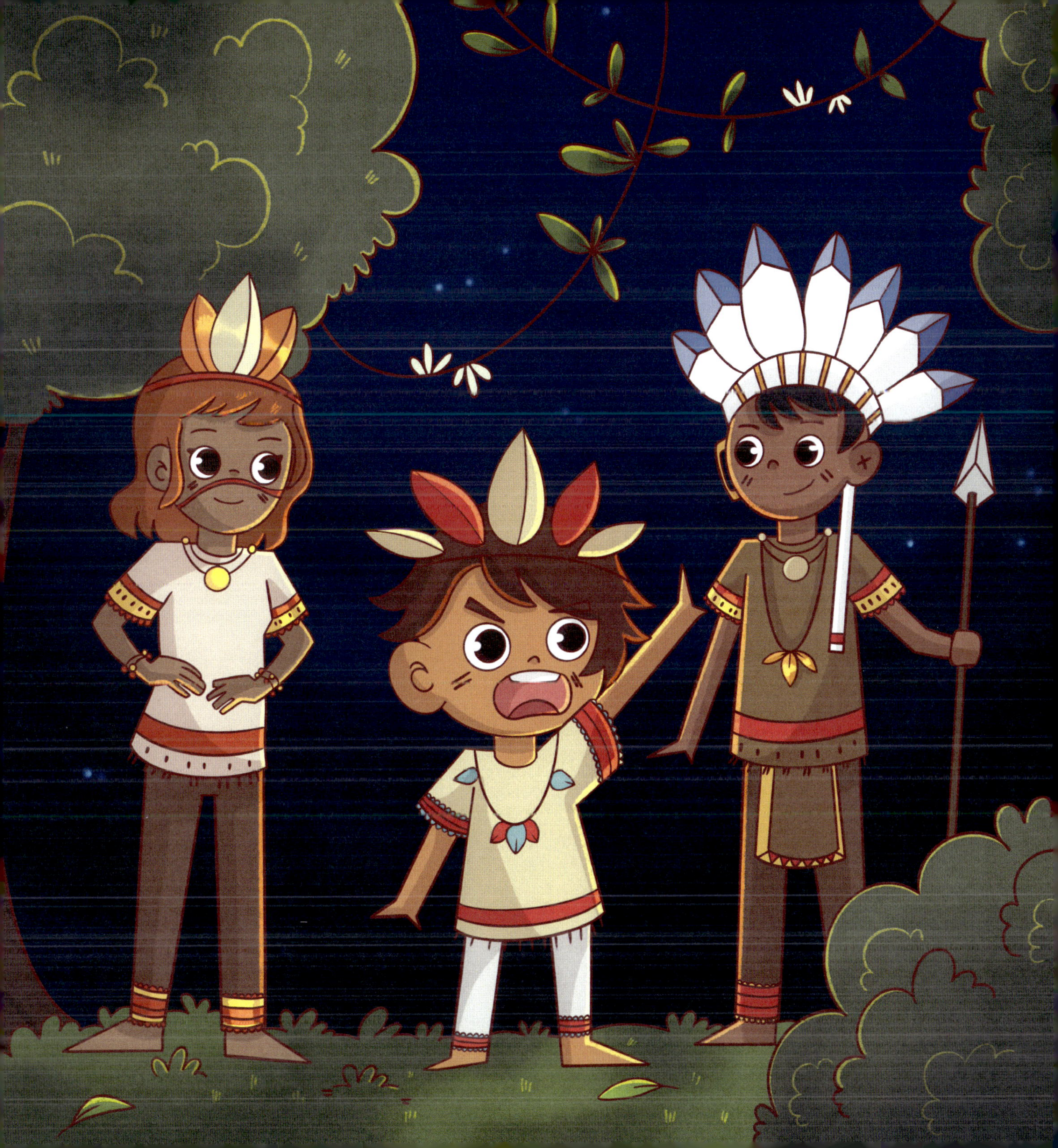

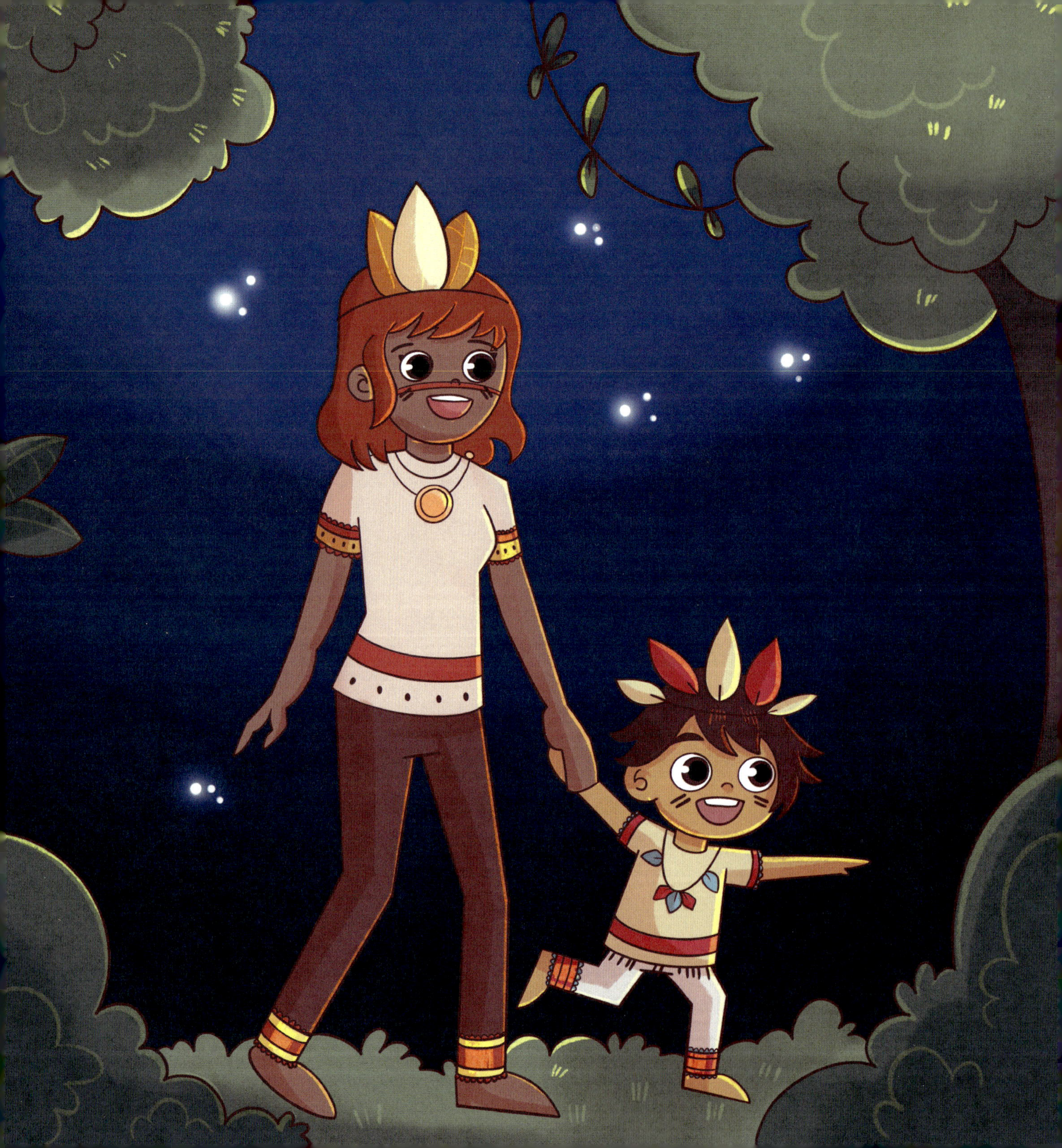

After a few moments, the boy is no longer sad or angry. He's not hungry anymore either.

He realizes the hunger was connected to the anger because both came up around dinnertime.

The boy's mother says, "At dinnertime, you want to play. Well, dinner is for sitting together as a family and eating. How about we play after dinner? What would you like to play?"

"Let's tell stories about our lives!" the boy exclaims.

The elder walks to the middle of the circle.

The entire tribe starts to clap and cheer.

The boy feels so happy.
He also feels close to his family and tribe.

The elder then summarizes as follows:

"Remember, anytime you are feeling something, you can practice the WAE."

A PART OF YOU FEELS THIS WAY . . .

WITNESS THE EMOTION.
Give it a color, a texture. Turn it into an animal.

ACCEPT THE EMOTION.
Ask what it is here to teach you. Aside from this, everything else is okay. This may reveal other emotions or thoughts. Accept them all until everything else is okay.

EXPRESS THE EMOTION.
Act like the animal would feeling this way. Dance, yell, cry, stamp your feet. There are many ways to release the emotions so they don't get stuck.

Once you are through the WAE,
you have witnessed, accepted, and
expressed the emotions. Then you will
find that what remains is joy and love.

**ALL EMOTIONS ARE SIMPLY SIGNS POINTING
THE WAY TOWARD JOY AND LOVE.**

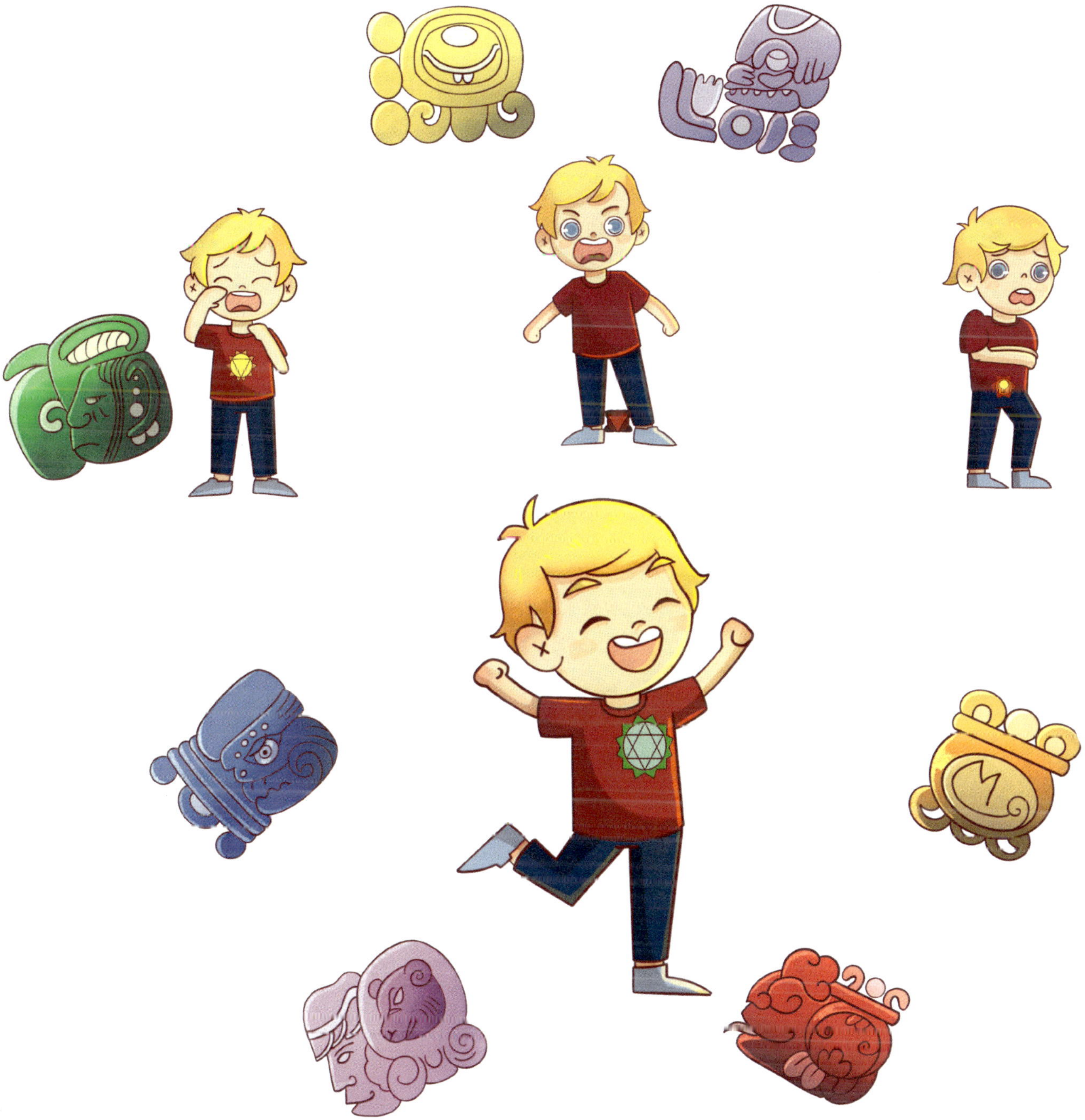

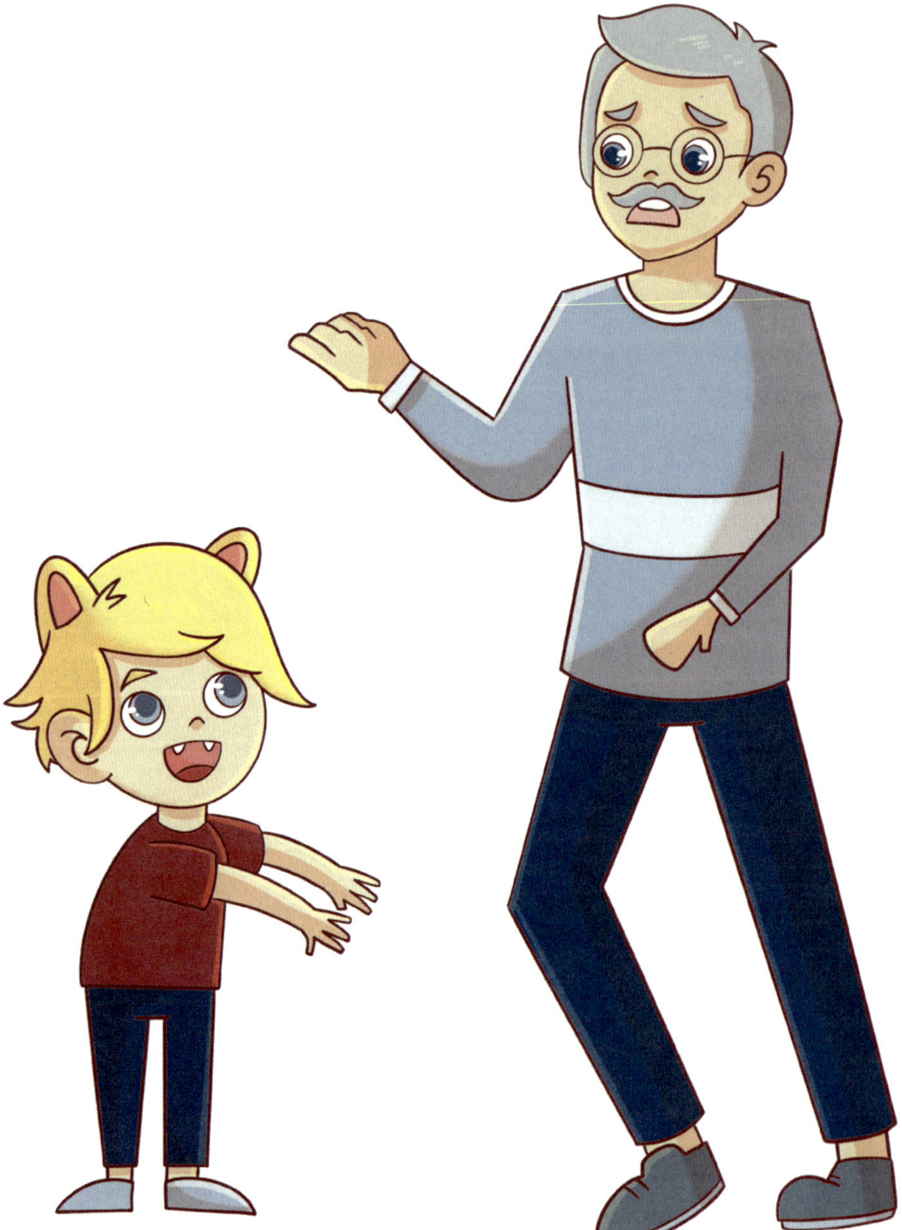

"SO, JAKE, WHAT
DO YOU THINK ABOUT
THIS STORY?"

"CAN I BE A
HAPPY TIGER?"

THE END

Made in the USA
Monee, IL
08 March 2025